KNOWLEDGE ENCYCLOPEDIA

MODERN ARCHITECTURE

© Wonder House Books 2025

All rights reserved. No part of this book may be reproduced or transmitted in any form by any means, electronic or mechanical, including photocopying and recording, or by any information storage and retrieval system except as may be expressly permitted in writing by the publisher.

Wonder House
(An imprint of Prakash Books)

contact@wonderhousebooks.com

Disclaimer: The information contained in this encyclopedia has been collated with inputs from subject experts. All information contained herein is true to the best of the Publisher's knowledge.

ISBN : 9789390391806

Table of Contents

Moving Towards Modernity	3
Baroque Grandeur	4–5
Baroque in Habsburg Lands	6–7
Baroque in Eastern Europe	8–9
Resplendent Rococo	10–11
Neoclassical Architecture	12–13
Classicism in the New World	14–15
Romanticism in Architecture	16–17
Gothic Revival	18–19
New-Age Iron and Glass	20–21
Beaux-Arts	22–23
Art Nouveau	24–25
Defying Tradition	26–27
Antoni Gaudí	28–29
Skyscrapers	30–31
Word Check	32

MOVING TOWARDS MODERNITY

From the 16th century onwards, exploration and empire-building brought new ideas and greater wealth to Europe. This gradually gave rise to an age where religious zeal was tempered by reason and science. One of the most remarkable gifts of advancing technology was its impact on architecture. Engineers and architects were able to look at new forms of construction that were previously unavailable to them. Sometimes it was because new solutions in mathematics and engineering came into being. Sometimes it was because of innovations in processing. Sometimes it was because they found new ways of using materials like iron, concrete, and steel. The plethora of choices combined with the unending imagination of architects gave rise to this brilliant new pre-modern era of architecture.

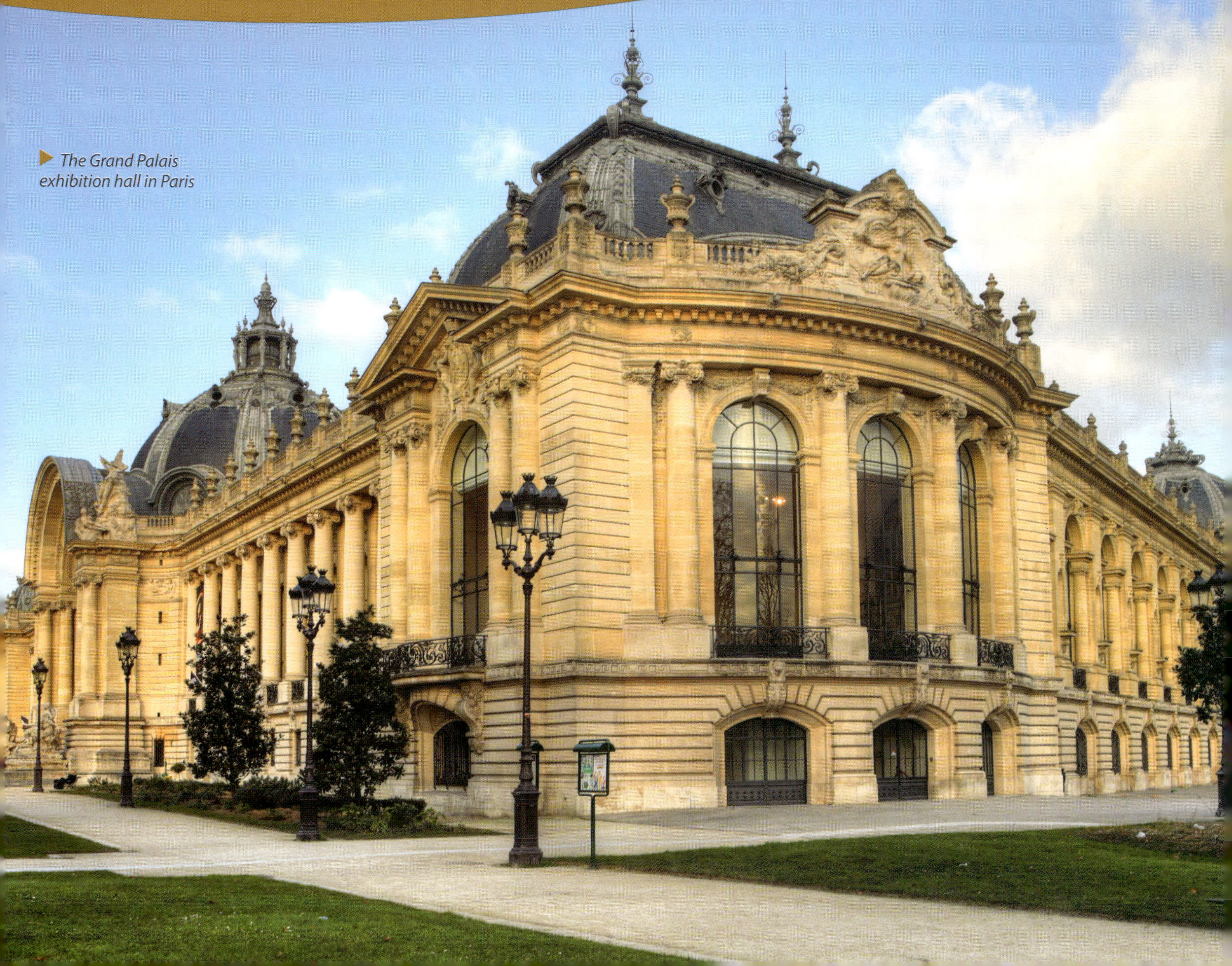

▶ *The Grand Palais exhibition hall in Paris*

Baroque Grandeur

In the late 16ᵗʰ century, Italian architects set aside the strictly proportional designs of the Renaissance era. Their compositions became more complex, detailed and sensual. This marked the start of the Baroque period, a time of grandiose and dramatic architecture that influenced buildings all across the West. In some places, like Germany and South America, it lasted until the 18ᵗʰ century.

▲ *The amazing, illusory frescoes seen under the dome of the Church of Gesù in Rome were created by Baroque artist Giovanni Battista Gaulli (also called 'Baciccio')*

▲ *St Paul's Cathedral is a masterpiece of English Baroque architecture created by astronomer, mathematician and one of England's most influential architects, Christopher Wren (1632–1723)*

Counter-Reformation

In the 16ᵗʰ century, many Christians had lost faith in the Catholic Church. A number of reformers came forth to change its practices, to remove its decadent and wrongful ways. Many of these reformers believed that art was a sin. But the Catholic Church knew how important art and architecture were to ordinary people. They understood that Christians needed holy places and divine paintings to feel close to God. Thus, they planned the Counter-Reformation movement. A key part of this plan was to use grand and powerful art and architecture to win back the people. The Baroque constructions were the result of Counter-Reformation.

▲ *Lying between curved, colonnaded arms, the vast Baroque square of St. Peter's Cathedral can hold thousands of people in its embrace. This is a symbol of the Catholic Church welcoming its faithful to the fold*

MODERN ARCHITECTURE

Baroque Styles

In keeping with the Catholic Church's wish to appeal to people's senses, baroque architecture was made to be vivid and fantastic. Architects built complex and palatial structures with richly embellished surfaces. Interiors were marked with twists and turns, dazzling displays of light, bright colours and sharp contrasts. Curved, gilded statues entwined with each other in weird and wonderful compositions. Walls and ceiling were covered with hypnotic, illusory paintings. Such imaginative grandeur had never before been seen. It was as much admired as criticised. 'Baroque' is sometimes used to mean extravagant, deformed and even absurd.

▶ *Adorning St. Michael's Church in Vienna is The Fall of the Angels (1781), a fabulous stucco relief sculpted by Austrian talent, Karl Georg Merville*

Palace of Versailles

Baroque architecture flowered into its most opulent forms in France. Nowhere is this more clearly visible than the spectacular Palace of Versailles built by Louis XIV (1638–1715), the Sun King. His royal residence was the combined effort of many brilliant men, including his favourite architect, Jules Hardouin-Mansart.

The palace's designs were typically Baroque in that their focus point was the interior, specifically the king's bedroom. From there, a series of divisions and repetitive motifs formed an awe-inspiring complex of buildings. This included two other palaces, the Grand Trianon and the Petit Trianon. Its symmetrical gardens, with their fountains of dragons, lions, nymphs and gods, were designed by the most influential landscape architect in French history, André Le Nôtre.

◀ *The king's bedchamber at the Palace of Versailles*

Isn't It Amazing!

Baroque architects thought of a building as a large sculpture. One of their chief talents, Francesco Borromini (1599–1667) designed ground plans for the Sant'Ivo alla Sapienza church to resemble a bee. This was to honour his patron, whose coat-of-arms featured bees.

▲ *Borromini's first independent commission was the quirky and imaginative San Carlo alle Quattro Fontane, completed in 1665 in Rome*

In Real Life

The most famous room in the Palace of Versailles is the Hall of Mirrors. Built over 1678–1689, this 70-metre-long gallery is lined with a series of large mirrors opposite equally large windows. Delicate glass chandeliers hang down from the arched, richly painted ceiling. Gilded statues and decorations cover the gallery. The entire effect is one of dazzling light and splendour.

▶ *The Hall of Mirrors*

Baroque in Habsburg Lands

For centuries, the House of Habsburg controlled Spain, Austria, Hungary, parts of the Netherlands, and many overseas colonies. At the time of Reformation, Charles V was the king of all these territories. He was also the Holy Roman Emperor, which made him a Catholic ally and supporter of the Counter-Reformation movement. Charles V's heirs continued in his footsteps and the Baroque period flourished throughout the Habsburg Empire.

▲ Designed by German architect Andreas Schluter and Danish amber craftsman Gottfried Wolfram, the Amber Room at Berlin City Palace was called the 'Eighth Wonder of the World'. Unfortunately, it did not survive WWII

▲ Located in the Grand Square of Sibiu, Brukenthal Palace (1777–1787) was the official home of the Habsburg Governor of Transylvania, Samuel von Brukenthal. In 1817, it became (and remains) one of the earliest museums in the world

Spain

Baroque styles from Italy began influencing Spain in the 17th century. Around 1667, talented men like Alonso Cano and Eufrasio Lopez de Rojas began adding Baroque-inspired motifs to the exteriors of Granada Cathedral and the Cathedral of Jaen, respectively. The celebrated Churriguera family of architects were most influential during the late 17th and early 18th centuries. Their name is synonymous with Spanish late-Baroque architecture. The intricate and exaggerated Churrigueresque style was later introduced to Mexico—a landmark structure being the Cathedral of Zacatecas—and to the Philippines.

▲ Churrigueresque grandeur at Granada Charterhouse's inner sanctuary

★ Incredible Individuals

Painter, sculptor, and architect Alonso Cano (1601–1667) produced religious works of such evocative strength, that he was dubbed the Spanish Michelangelo. Cano led a tumultuous life. In 1638, he fled Seville after a duel with an artist. In 1644, he escaped again when he was suspected of murdering his wife. Cano later took holy orders and became the chief architect of Granada Cathedral until his death.

▲ Granada Cathedral's Baroque facade was designed by Alonso Cano

Hungary

Built by Pietro Spozzo over 1629–1637, the Jesuit Church of Nagyszombat is perhaps the first great Baroque building in Hungary. During the 17th and 18th centuries, Jesuit patrons used the Baroque style to rebuild areas conquered from the **Ottoman Empire**. This included townscapes of places like Gyor (1630s), Kosice (1670s), Eger (1730s) and Szekesfehervar (1740s). The Royal Palace in Buda, Grassalkovich Castle in Godollo, and Esterhazy Castle in Fertod are the nation's most important Baroque structures.

▲ Buda Castle, the massive home of Hungarian kings, rises from the banks of the River Danube and towers over the city

The Low Countries

Joining the spirit of the Counter-Reformation movement, the Catholic churches in the southern region of the Low Countries set up many important architectural projects. Perhaps the most famous Flemish architect of this period is Wenzel Coebergher. He trained in Italy and is best-known for the heptagonal (seven-sided) Basilica of Our Fair Lady of Scherpenheuvel.

◀ Spanish, French, and Dutch Baroque aesthetics come together in the Abbey of Averbode (1667) in Belgium

In Real Life

The Marian cult of Scherpenheuvel began when the villagers of Zichem flocked to worship a statue of the Virgin Mary on an oak tree upon a hill. The shrine took on its beautiful Baroque shape under the patronage of the Habsburg rulers Ferdinand and Isabella. It is said to be the most popular pilgrimage site in Belgium.

The Holy Roman Empire

In the early days, master masons from Italy and Switzerland dominated the baroque scene. Over the 17th century, Austria developed its own style. The Austrian architect Johann Fischer von Erlach combined elements of Classical and Baroque styles, forming a new style popular with the Imperial power. After him, military engineer Johann Lucas von Hildebrandt became the leading court architect. The empire also adopted French palace architecture, particularly, the horseshoe-like layout, enclosing a courtyard on the town side. The outstanding German palace of this period was the Würzburg Residence. It blends Austro-Italian and French designs.

▼ Baroque glamour in Germany's spectacular Würzburg Residence

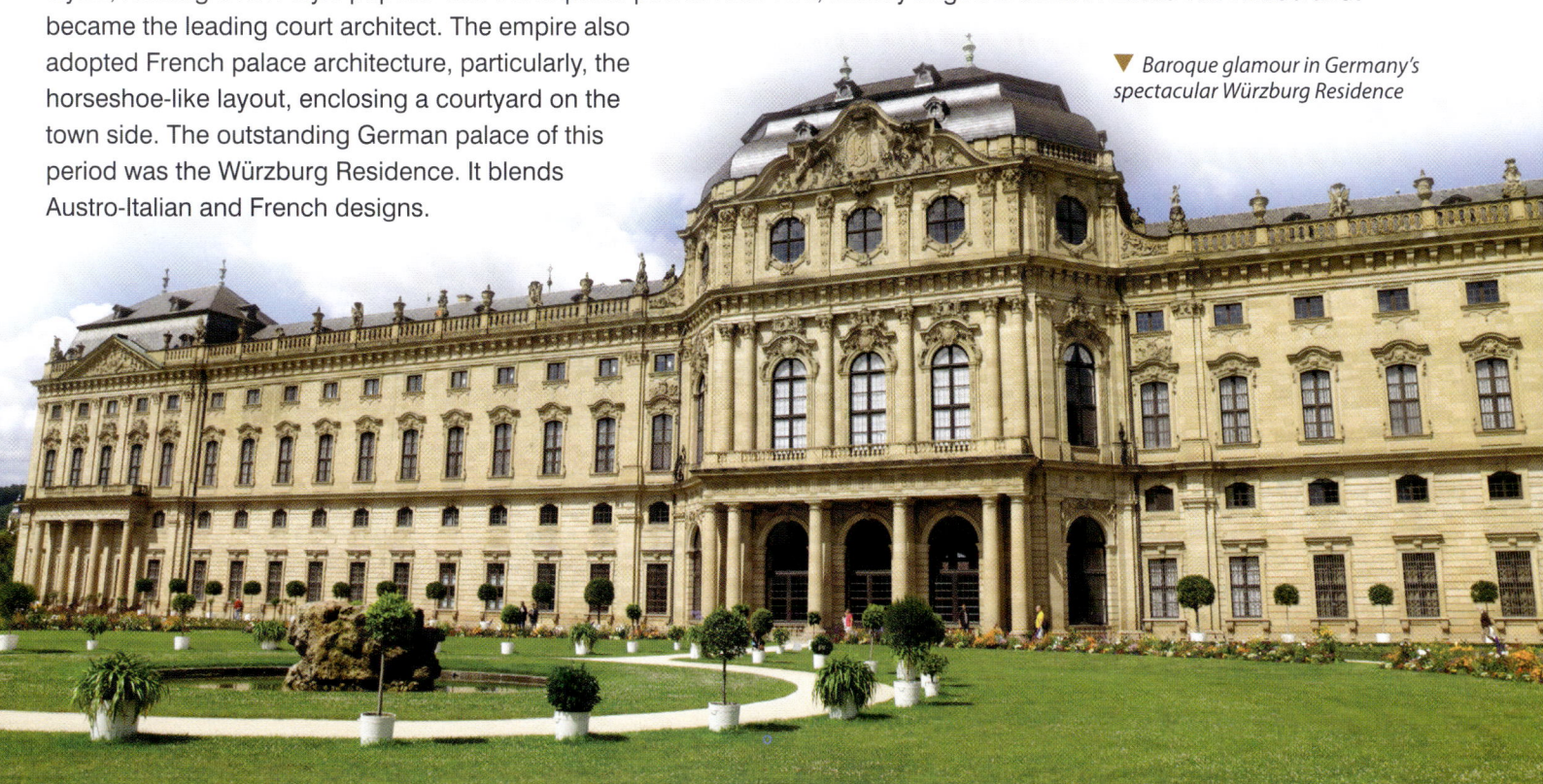

Baroque in Eastern Europe

The German-Baroque touch spread to Poland, the Baltic States, and Russia. The early Russian style, seen at the end of the 17th century, is called Naryshkin Baroque. It is marked by elegant white ornamentation on red-brick walls, usually at churches. The style changed under Dutch influence into Petrine Baroque. It was named after the nation's powerful monarch, Peter the Great. The period culminated in the opulent Rastrelli style. Named after architect Bartolomeo Francesco Rastrelli, this style combined elements of Rococo with Russian aesthetics to produce amazing, multicoloured structures. Favoured by the Russian empresses Anna I and Elizabeth I, Rastrelli erected numerous palaces for members of the imperial court fir over 50 years.

▲ Naryshkin Baroque was originally seen in the Church of the Intercession of the Virgin at Fili (1693), on the estate of the boyar Naryshkin

▲ This painting by Konstantin Ukhtomsky shows the Jordan Staircase, one of Rastrelli's 18th-century masterpieces at the sumptuous Winter Palace

Petrine Russia

Tsar Peter the Great (1672–1725) inherited a love for art and architecture from both sides of his family, Naryshkin and Romanov. When he came to power, he dedicated a lot of time and resources to building St. Petersburg into a grand centre for culture and scholarship. Every building erected there had to first meet his design approval, in particular, his palaces and gardens that were constructed by the sea. Most buildings at this time were made with brick or stone to lower the risk of fire. This gave rise to a city that embodied a new Russian expression of scale, colour, and form. It rapidly spread to other parts of the country, where it developed regional variations. Unfortunately, much of this Petrine Baroque architecture was destroyed during the 20th century.

⭐ Incredible Individuals

Rastrelli's style attracted so many followers, it led to a distinct school of architecture. In 1749, Prince Dmitry Ukhtomsky (1717–1774), a student of Rastrelli's, established one of the earliest Russian architectural colleges in Moscow.

▲ Rastrelli's spectacular ballroom in Catherine Palace

◄ Located on the Neva riverfront, the turreted Kunstkamera is Russia's first museum. Established by Peter the Great, the building was designed by German architect Georg Johann Mattarnovy and constructed over 1719–1727

MODERN ARCHITECTURE

Peterhof Palace

After a visit to the French court in 1717, Peter the Great commissioned the Peterhof Palace to rival the royal residence at Versailles. The largest of its palaces, the Grand Palace, was designed by Domenico Trezzini from 1714–1728. The gardens were planned by Alexandre Le Blond. In 1752, Bartolomeo Rastrelli made the palace even larger, thus making it the most opulent summer residence of the Russian royalty.

▲ Exquisite statues of gold adorn the steps and the grand cascade of fountains in front of Peterhof Palace

The Polish-Lithuanian Commonwealth

The Kingdom of Poland and the Grand Duchy of Lithuania were ruled by a single Catholic monarch. Thus, both nations were early adopters of Counter-Reformation and the Baroque forms. The commonwealth's oldest Baroque church is the 1587 Corpus Christi Church in Nesvizh, Belarus. It also has the oldest domed basilica with a Baroque exterior. This period was influenced by Eastern, specifically Ottoman, ideals. The German architect Johann Christoph Glaubitz (1700–1767) developed a distinct and popular Vilnius Baroque style, best seen today in the old town of Vilnius.

Towards the end of the century, the influence of Polish Baroque could be seen in the **Cossack Hetmanate**. Here, the style is combined with Orthodox architecture to give rise to the unique and popular Ukrainian Baroque style of architecture.

▲ The 18th-century Visitation of Our Lady Basilica at Wambierzyce, a beloved pilgrimage site in Poland

Christoph Dientzenhofer

The Bavarian architect Christoph Dientzenhofer (1655–1722) was a leading architect of the Bohemian Baroque style. He transformed Prague and Bohemia with his boldly designed buildings.

▶ Built by Dientzenhofer and his talented son, Brevnov Monastery is a flowing structure of curved walls and intersecting oval spaces

Resplendent Rococo

In France, high Baroque aesthetic was combined with a delicate, decorative form of art and architecture to produce Rococo. This style came into being after the death of Louis XIV and flourished until the French Revolution. Though primarily associated with France, it spread to other parts of Europe for a short time. Rococo is more light and charming than the grand and ponderous Baroque. Where Baroque architects designed horizontally separate structures, Rococo architects created unified spaces. This allowed them to produce continuous themes in decoration.

▲ Delicate 18th-century decorations on the walls of the French Prime Minister's office at Hotel Matignon

▲ The Hall of Mirrors at Amalienburg is a grandiose 18th-century hunting lodge in southern Germany

Louis XV Period

Rococo opulence is sometimes seen as a symbol of the decadence that existed in the years before the French Revolution. It reached its peak during the long reign of Louis XV (r. 1715–1774). For this reason, interior designs and furniture pieces from this time are said to belong to the 'Louis XV period'. Unlike the Catholic Baroque, Rococo took place in an age of growing secularism. It was aimed at pleasing the senses using asymmetric, often **arabesque** schemes. The style was pioneered and developed by interior designers, artists and craftsmen such as Nicolas Pineau (1684–1754), Juste-Aurele Meissonnier (c. 1693–1750) and Pierre Le Pautre (1659–1744). The fashionable interiors of the Chateau de Chantilly (c. 1722) and Hotel de Soubise in Paris (c. 1732) mark the high point of the Louis XV period.

▲ The ceiling of the Salon de la Princesse in Hotel de Soubise, Paris

Isn't It Amazing!

The castle in the Disney movie *Beauty and the Beast* was inspired by Rococo. Lumiere, the enchanted candlestick, bears a striking resemblance to the works of J. A. Meissonnier, in particular the goldsmith's iconic candelabra from around 1735.

▶ Meissonnier's famous silver candlestick resembles twists of leaves and flowers

MODERN ARCHITECTURE

Rococo Affectations

Lavish Rococo combined two styles—the French Rocaille, a delicate, symmetrical form of decoration inspired by nature, and the heavy Italian Barocco (Baroque). The French word *rocaille* refers to shells, rocks, and similar-shaped knick-knacks that adorned grottoes and bordered fountains. Other common themes included fish, birds, bees, climbers, leaves, and flowers. The homes of the well-to-do were cluttered with clocks, frames, mirrors, candlesticks, and furniture that employed this form of ornamentation. Decorative statuary and paintings were thus an integral part of Rococo architecture.

Chinoiserie

First appearing in the 17th century, *chinoiserie* is the interpretation of Chinese motifs in Western art. Stylised dragons and phoenixes were popular during the Rococo period. Structures like the Chinese House in Potsdam, Germany and the Chinese Village in Tsarskoye Selo, Russia, were built in a mix of Rococo and *chinoiserie* style.

▲ The Rocaille wall clock (c. 1745–1750) is shaped like a shell. It is the work of watchmaker Ferdinand Berthoud and sculptor Jacques Caffieri

▲ Porcelain from Vincennes, France depicting a Chinese rural scene

◀ Designed by Johann Gottfried Buring, the Chinese House was built by Fredrick II of Prussia in a garden of his summer palace. It served as a teahouse

Rococo in Europe

Rococo architecture became immensely popular in Eastern Europe and Russia. Western Europe more easily accepted its interior fashions. The abbey church, built by the Asam brothers in Weltenburg, Germany, is typically theatrical with its oval simplicity offset by rich white-and-gold ornamentation. Beyond the high altar is an amazing sculpture of St. George spearing a writhing dragon. Flemish architect Jaime Borty Milia introduced Rococo to Spain when he constructed the west facade of the Cathedral of Murcia in 1733. Spanish Rococo found its greatest champion in Ventura Rodríguez, who created the dazzling interiors of the Basilica of Our Lady of the Pillar in Saragossa (1750).

▲ Weltenburg Abbey's Rococo interior with its famous sculpture of St. George and the dragon

◀ The extraordinary hanging sculpture at the high altar of the former monastery Rohr, in Germany, was created by Egid Quirin Asam (1692–1750)

Neoclassical Architecture

Classical architecture refers to ancient Greek and Roman constructions. The style was revived and further developed during the Renaissance period between the 14th and 16th centuries. When it flourished again during 1750–1830, it was described as the 'true style'. In later days, it came to be known as Neoclassicism. At this time, people were exploring, digging, and discovering Classical sites in Italy, Greece, and Asia Minor. This naturally led to a renewed interest in Classical studies, which coincided with the European **Age of Reason**. The movement was marked by a search for architectural truth. It rose against the illusion, ornament, and exaggeration of the Baroque and Rococo eras.

▲ The Konzerthaus (concert hall) on Gendarmenmarkt square is one of many architectural gems designed for Berlin by city planner Karl Friedrich Schinkel (1781–1841)

▲ Tired of Rastrelli excesses, Queen Catherine the Great (c. 1762–1796) of Russia summoned Scottish architect Charles Cameron (1745–1812) to build the Neoclassical Pavlovsk Palace in Saint Petersburg

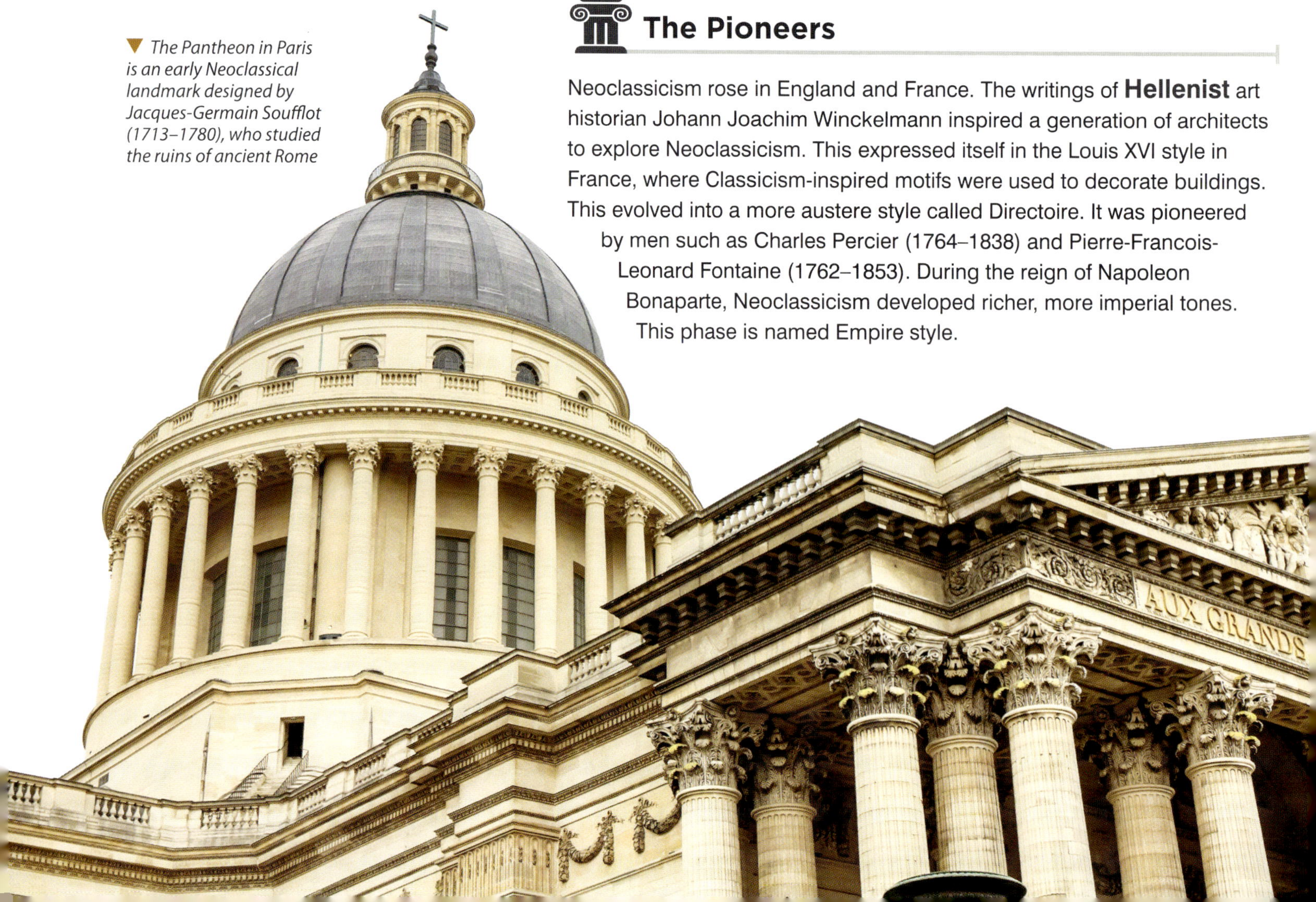

▼ The Pantheon in Paris is an early Neoclassical landmark designed by Jacques-Germain Soufflot (1713–1780), who studied the ruins of ancient Rome

The Pioneers

Neoclassicism rose in England and France. The writings of **Hellenist** art historian Johann Joachim Winckelmann inspired a generation of architects to explore Neoclassicism. This expressed itself in the Louis XVI style in France, where Classicism-inspired motifs were used to decorate buildings. This evolved into a more austere style called Directoire. It was pioneered by men such as Charles Percier (1764–1838) and Pierre-Francois-Leonard Fontaine (1762–1853). During the reign of Napoleon Bonaparte, Neoclassicism developed richer, more imperial tones. This phase is named Empire style.

MODERN ARCHITECTURE

Neoclassicism in Britain

The British Isles used imposing Neoclassical designs to construct public buildings such as banks, museums, and post offices. Notably, John Soane (1753–1837) designed the Bank of England and Robert Smirke (1780–1867) created the British Museum, the General Post Office, and Covent Garden Theatre. Possibly the most famous architect of this time was John Nash (1752–1835). His designs for parks and city blocks changed the appearance of London. Among his creations are Regent's Park, Carlton House Terrace, and the Buckingham Palace.

Incredible Individuals

The Arc de Triomphe in Paris was commissioned by Napoleon Bonaparte in 1806 to commemorate his victory in Austerlitz. Based on ancient Roman arches, this ostentatious structure was finished only in 1836, 25 years after the death of its architect, Jean Chalgrin.

▲ The world's largest freestanding triumphal arch, the Arc de Triomphe, Paris

▲ The Neoclassical facade and palatial extension of Buckingham House was commissioned by King George IV (1762–1830) and designed by John Nash

Palladianism

Andrea Palladio (1508–1580) was one of the greatest architects during the late Renaissance period. His theories of rationality, order, and symmetry in buildings heavily influenced Neoclassical architects. The resulting movement was called Palladianism. The first Palladian house of the 18th century was Wilbury House, built in Wiltshire by William Benson, a member of Parliament. Champions of the style included the Scottish architect and publisher Colen Campbell (1676–1729), Richard Boyle, third Earl of Burlington (1694–1753), and his protégé William Kent (c. 1685–1748).

▲ Burlington's home, Chiswick House, was inspired by Palladio's famous Villa Rotunda

▲ One of Colen Campbell's impeccable Palladian creations, Houghton Hall in Norfolk was commissioned by Robert Walpole, who is regarded as Great Britain's first Prime Minister

▲ In 1769, George Dance the Younger modified London's Newgate Prison along Palladian lines. The imaginative new building had grim drama and was one of the city's most original constructions until it was demolished in 1902

Classicism in the New World

Neoclassical architecture found its true home in the Americas. A notable early architect of the style was the third President of the USA, Thomas Jefferson (1743–1826). He famously created the Virginia State Capitol and his own home, Monticello ("little mountain"). During the 19th century, the newly formed USA built many public buildings, even universities, in the Neoclassical style. In Latin America too, military engineers and urban architects built imposing public structures such as hospitals, prisons, banks, and post offices. As a result, many nations of the New World closely identify with Classical aesthetics.

▲ In 1844, a fire swept through the Cathedral of Arequipa in Peru. Architect Lucas Poblete rebuilt and expanded the cathedral into a unique structure, incorporating the triumphal arch motif from Classical canons

▲ The symmetrical and refined La Moneda Palace in Santiago is the seat of the President of Chile. It was built around a series of vast courtyards in the late 18th century by architect Joaquin Toesca y Ricci

The Federal Style

The Classical theories of ancient Rome resonated with the ideals of the new US republic. Neoclassical designs seen in this young nation, especially over 1785–1815, are called Federalist. The style originated with the works of Jefferson, Benjamin Latrobe (1764–1820), and Charles Bulfinch (1763–1844). The architecture is marked by plain and austere surfaces. It carries Classical motifs like panels, tablets, and friezes. The ruins of ancient Roman towns around Mount Vesuvius, such as Pompeii and Herculaneum, deeply influenced Federalist styles.

▲ Elfreth's Alley is a historical street in Philadelphia. It is famous for its Federalist-style homes, built over the 18th century for shipwrights, furniture craftsmen, glass-blowers, silversmiths, and other tradespeople

In Real Life

Designed by Jefferson, the Virginia State Capitol is the first public building in the US to be modelled entirely on a Roman temple, specifically the 1st century Maison Carrée in southern France. Designed in partnership with Charles-Louis Clérisseau (1721–1820), the stucco-clad brick building took almost two decades to build and was further added to during the 19th century.

▲ This 1865 photo shows the Capitol building in Richmond, Virginia, in Jefferson's original design, before it was renovated and expanded

MODERN ARCHITECTURE

Massachusetts State House

A landmark building designed by Bulfinch is the Massachusetts State House (1795–1797). It was inspired by London's Somerset House, an amazing Neoclassical mansion created by Scottish-Swedish architect William Chambers. The Massachusetts State House is remarkable for its main dome. This central feature was so well-liked, it became a standard part of most other state-capitol designs.

▲ The famous wooden dome of the Massachusetts State House was gilded at great expense during the late 1990s

The Egyptian Obsession

American Neoclassicism was also fascinated and influenced by ancient Egypt. Between 1848–1888, America built the colossal obelisk—a structure from ancient Egypt and Rome—called the Washington Monument. It was also the tallest structure in the world until the Eiffel Tower was built. At just over 169 metres, it remains the tallest structure made of stone and the tallest obelisk in the world.

◀ Sunrise over the Egypt-inspired Washington Monument, located beside the Greek-inspired Lincoln Memorial, with the Rome-inspired Capitol Building in the distance

Capitol Building, Washington, D.C.

The US Capitol Building was designed by the physician Dr William Thornton (1759–1828). His plan showed a grand entrance with projecting horizontal wings. The central building rose on vertical columns and was crowned by a magnificent dome. Some of these structures were built out of wood and later rebuilt using stone and iron. Since Thornton was not an architect, a number of more formally trained men oversaw the actual construction. This included Benjamin Latrobe and Charles Bulfinch, who added their own designs to Thornton's plans. The cornerstone was laid by President Washington on September 18, 1793. Construction continued well into the 19th century, while much renovation and modernisation took place in the 20th century. Today, the awe-inspiring Neoclassical facade and dome of the Capitol are among the most recognisable American icons.

▲ The eastern facade of the US Capitol Building, Washington, D.C., with its spectacular central dome

Romanticism in Architecture

During the 19th century, Europe was wealthy and changing rapidly. New territories were being conquered overseas, and through the returning ships, new influences swept into the continent. While the exotic was eagerly adopted, Europe eventually became nostalgic for its older, home-grown styles. The resulting architectural revival was marked by a romantic remembrance of those styles, rather than a strict adherence to the original. Neoclassicism and Gothic Revival were major parts of this Romanticism. Buildings were also constructed in Baroque Revival and Romanesque Revival, and influenced by Indian, Chinese, Egyptian, and Moorish designs. Romanticism saw the rise of fantastic, whimsical architecture that combined the exotic with native sensibilities.

▲ A riot of red, blue, and yellow, the domed and turreted Palacio da Pena in Portugal was built with a mix of Moorish, Manueline, and medieval motifs

▲ Russian Revival was a melding of Byzantine and early Russian Baroque styles. This gave rise to buildings as varied as (from left to right) the Church of the Dormition, the Great Kremlin Palace, and the Cathedral of Saints Peter and Paul

Gründerzeit

In Germany, Gründerzeit (meaning, founding period) refers to the prosperous times after the Franco-Prussian War of 1870–1871 and the founding of the German Empire in 1871. It was marked by a renewed interest in Germanic heritage. The well-to-do middle class showed off their new-found wealth with richly decorated and furnished houses. This is particularly seen in the works of Max Arwed Rossbach, who was inspired by historic architectural styles.

▶ The unique Palais Rossbach is an architectural jewel of Leipzig, Germany

Incredible Individuals

In the 1870s, Russian architects looked to their folk culture for inspiration. They glorified peasant architecture and created vivid and intricately decorated palaces and towers of wood. This Russian Revival style was founded by the brilliant Ivan Ropet. Sadly, few of these wonders remain today.

MODERN ARCHITECTURE

Fairytale Castles

In the early 19th century, the Grimm Brothers published their famous collection of gothic folktales. Inspired by such fairytales, new castle-like buildings cropped up with turrets, pinnacles, small windows and wonky roofs. The most amazing fairytale castle is Neuschwanstein in Germany. Built by King Ludwig II of Bavaria, this dreamy palace is nestled in forested mountains that overlook a sheer gorge. The castle came from an imaginative painting by stage designer and painter, Christian Jank (1833–1888). It was turned into an architecturally sound Romanesque plan by Eduard Riedel (1813–1885). In 1874, Georg von Dollmann became the castle's chief architect; he was replaced by Julius Hofmann in 1886.

Incredible Individuals

Ludwig II of Bavaria, nicknamed "Mad King Ludwig", preferred spending his time on the arts rather than deal with affairs of the state. Apart from his four castles, he is also famous for his patronage of the gifted German composer Richard Wagner. Though Ludwig was much loved by his people, the politicians despised him. He was ultimately declared insane and removed from the throne. Three days later, he was found drowned under mysterious circumstances.

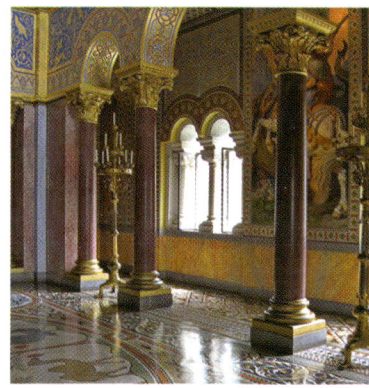
◀ This detail from the lavish Throne Room at Neuschwanstein shows Byzantine motifs inspired by the Hagia Sophia (in modern-day Istanbul)

◀ Neuschwanstein was the inspiration behind the Sleeping Beauty Castle in Disneyland

The Brighton Pavilion

In the 18th century, the seaside town of Brighton was a popular resort for the rich. Prince George (later, King George IV of Great Britain) hired an architect named Henry Holland (1745–1806) to rebuild his Brighton home into a villa. But the project rapidly grew in scope. The Prince, who was fascinated by the mysterious East, imported lavish furnishings, curios, and hand-painted wallpapers from China. In 1815, he handed over the project to John Nash, who transformed the house into a fantastic oriental palace. Nash turned the exterior into an Indian-inspired conglomeration of minarets and domes. The palace even used cast iron during its construction. Inside, it was an opulent labyrinth of rooms, corridors, and galleries.

▼ George IV's Royal Pavilion at Brighton

Gothic Revival

Gothic Revival was one of the most influential movements of the 18th century. It came about through the influence of Romantic literature in England. At this time, dramatic novels and poems with Gothic themes were popular. They inspired both the aristocracy and the wealthy middle class. People who had the time and means to indulge their fantasies began to commission Gothic-inspired buildings. Houses with castle-like battlements and turrets began cropping up all over England, especially towards the end of the century. The style soon spread to Europe, North America, and even Australia.

▲ St. Paul's Cathedral in Melbourne, Australia was designed by the English Gothic Revival architect William Butterfield towards the end of the 19th century

▲ Church of Saint Peter and Saint Paul at Ostend, Belgium, created in Gothic Revival during 1899–1908

▼ The Basilica of Saint Clotilde is perhaps Paris's first great neo-Gothic structure. It was designed by architect François-Christian Gau (1790–1853) and completed by his partner Théodore Ballu by 1857

Neo-Gothic Architecture

The 19th century saw the rise of a more serious and studied Gothic style of architecture. This was closer to the original medieval version. It is sometimes called neo-Gothic, to set it apart from the earlier, more frivolous forms of Gothic Revival. Neo-Gothic had a significant impact on the landscape of Europe and North America. With centuries of advances in building technology, more Gothic structures were constructed during the 19th and 20th centuries than during medieval times.

Incredible Individuals

Gothic Revivalism became a trend after the English writer Horace Walpole (1717–1797) published his medieval thriller, *The Castle of Otranto*. Walpole's own home, Strawberry Hill, was modified over several years by several architects. It is a fanciful Gothic-inspired estate with artificial ruins, asymmetrical buildings, towers, stained-glass windows, and even elements of chinoiserie and Rococo.

▶ A section of Horace Walpole's Gothic Revival home, Strawberry Hill

MODERN ARCHITECTURE

 ## The Palace of Westminster

Located on the north bank of the River Thames, the beautiful Palace of Westminster has been the meeting place for the Parliament of the UK since the 13th century. The structure was almost destroyed by a huge fire in 1834. The reconstruction of the palace was turned into an architectural competition. The person with the winning design was Charles Barry (1795–1860). He planned the new buildings in the Gothic Revival style. Most of what remained of the old palace became a part of this new, much larger construction. The palace now holds over 1,100 rooms which are laid out symmetrically around two series of courtyards. The iconic structure of the new palace is the Elizabeth Tower, better known by the nickname of its Great Bell—Big Ben.

▲ The Great Bell of Big Ben weighs 13,760 kilograms, and is 2.28 metres tall and 2.75 metres wide

 ## The Gothic Skyscraper

With the 20th century came amazing technologies such as light bulbs and lifts. At the same time, steel replaced stone as the main load-bearing material. Some architects combined steel frameworks with decorative Gothic motifs to create incredible, new age buildings. This can be seen in architect Cass Gilbert's 1913 skyscraper, the Woolworth Building in New York.

◀ For almost 20 years, the Woolworth Building was the world's tallest skyscraper. Despite its Gothic ornamentation, it represented cutting-edge architecture with the most advanced system of lifts

In Real Life

The Palace of Westminster was bombed on 14 different occasions during WWII. Many parts of it, such as the Commons Chamber, had to be reconstructed after the war. The building also underwent massive conservation work to reverse the effects of air pollution.

▲ Charles Barry's Commons Chamber was destroyed by German bombs during WWII

New-Age Iron and Glass

In the 19th and early 20th centuries, inventors were making fascinating machines which allowed for mass production of goods. As machines became part of the workforce, new types of buildings were constructed to accommodate them. These included different kinds of factories, power plants, warehouses, department stores, offices, and exhibition halls, to name just a few. New infrastructure, capable of handling machines, also had to be built. Hangars, garages, telephone stations, railway and bus stations; and new types of bridges, tunnels, and roads were needed. Architects and engineers of this booming industrial time invented amazing techniques using iron, steel, glass, and concrete. In 1851, Sir Joseph Paxton's landmark Crystal Palace in London showed how iron and glass could be used to build delicate yet lofty spaces.

▲ Penn Station, New York, around 1936

▲ Henri Labrouste's extraordinary nine-domed iron-and-glass reading room (1860–1867) at the Bibliothèque Nationale, Paris

◀ Constructed by Abraham Darby III over 1777–1779, Iron Bridge is the world's first major cast-iron bridge. It runs across the River Severn in Shropshire, England, and is now closed to vehicles but still used by pedestrians

Crystal Palace, London

Designed by Sir Joseph Paxton, the Crystal Palace was a building made entirely of wrought-iron, with walls made of 300,000 panes of glass. The main body was 563 metres long, 124 metres wide, and 33 metres high at its centre. It had a floor area of about 92,000 m², which drew about 14,000 British and international exhibitors. Among the fascinating things on display were false teeth, steam engines, Colt's repeating pistol, the Koh-i-Noor and Daria-i-Noor diamonds, and many other raw and finished products.

▲ The Crystal Palace in Hyde Park, London

MODERN ARCHITECTURE

The Eiffel Tower

Built over 1887–1889, the Eiffel Tower was built in preparation of the Exposition Universelle held in Paris in 1889. The event marked the 100th year of the French Revolution. The company that built the tower was owned by the engineer Gustave Eiffel. The tower was originally designed by Maurice Koechlin and Emile Nouguier, two engineers working in Eiffel's company. Stephen Sauvestre, the company's head architect, added decorative motifs, including the arches at the base and the glass pavilion on the first level. The Eiffel Tower is made of 18,038 metal parts and 7,300 tons of iron. It was built by 150–300 workers on the site, apart from the 50 engineers and designers.

Isn't It Amazing!

At 324 metres, the Eiffel Tower was the tallest structure in the world until 1930, when the Chrysler Building was erected in New York. The tower is not always this high, though. In cold weather, it shrinks by about 6 inches.

▶ As a notable engineer, Gustave Eiffel also contributed to building the Statue of Liberty

▲ The Eiffel Tower was supposed to be a temporary structure and was scheduled to be dismantled in 1909!

A Chocolate Factory

Menier Chocolate was a chocolate-producing company founded in France in 1816, when chocolate was often used as a medicinal product. During the 1860s, they hired architect Jules Saulnier (1817–1881) to create new buildings for the expanding business. One of these, the Turbine mill, built in 1871 is the first building to have a fully iron skeleton. The infill walls were non-load-bearing. The building was constructed directly over the River Marne and beautifully painted in patterns of yellow-browns and grey-blues. This iconic construction of the Industrial Era is now on the tentative list of UNESCO to be named a World Heritage Site.

▲ The amazing Saulnier building of the Menier Chocolate Factory

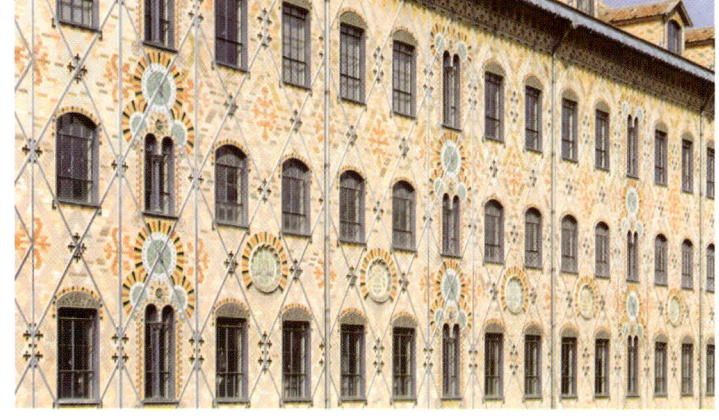

Beaux-Arts

The Ecole des Beaux-Arts (School of Fine Arts) in Paris gave its name to an amazing form of architecture that flourished over the 19th and early 20th centuries. Beaux-Arts architecture was inspired by Neoclassicism, but broke free from its most severe forms. It did so by using Gothic elements and industrial-age materials like glass, wrought-iron, and steel. The style became immensely popular in the Americas. In the USA, it was promoted by numerous American architects who had studied at the Beaux-Arts school. This included the celebrated Henry Hobson Richardson.

▲ Built at the end of the 19th century, the Water Company Palace (Palacio de Aguas Corrientes) is a Beaux-Arts gem of Buenos Aires, Argentina

 ## Grand Palais des Champs-Élysées

This Beaux-Arts work was built by the architects Albert Louvet, Henri Deglane, Albert Thomas, and Charles Girault. The exhibition hall and museum is a vaulting, modern structure of glass, iron, and steel hidden behind an ornate stone facade.

▶ The entrance to the Grand Palais, with its glass and metal domes rising behind

 ## Origins of Beaux-Arts

The formality of Neoclassicism fell out of favour with some teachers at the French academy. This included men like Joseph-Louis Duc (1802–1879), Henri Labrouste (1801–1875) and Leon Vaudoyer (1803–1872). Around this time, there was a renewed interest in the Middle Ages. By including elements from the Middle Ages, the architects wanted to create a more original French style of architecture. Breaking away from Rome, they wished to produce architecture imbued with their own national character.

▲ Setting the trend for modern library architecture, Henri Labrouste's Bibliothèque Nationale de France

▲ Sainte-Geneviève Library in Paris looks austerely. Classical on the outside, it is full of innovative and glorious metalwork and glass-work inside

MODERN ARCHITECTURE

▲ One of the two amazing Fontaines de la Concorde in the Place de la Concorde, Paris. Designed by Jacques Hittorff, it was finished in 1840 (during the reign of King Louis-Philippe)

Beaux-Arts in the USA

In America, Beaux-Arts is more closely associated with Greco-Roman revivalism. Over 1880–1930, it led to some of the most lofty, extravagant, and awe-inspiring buildings in the country. Beaux-Arts set trends for modern America by constructing public structures that are still in use today. This includes museums, universities, and even railway stations. Early architects of the style include the gifted Richard Morris Hunt and Henry Hobson Richardson. They brought the style back to the USA and inspired a generation of eager architectural students.

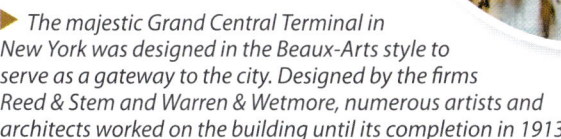

▶ The majestic Grand Central Terminal in New York was designed in the Beaux-Arts style to serve as a gateway to the city. Designed by the firms Reed & Stem and Warren & Wetmore, numerous artists and architects worked on the building until its completion in 1913

▲ Designed by Richard Morris Hunt and completed at the turn of the 20th century, the Great Hall is part of the Beaux-Arts building of the Metropolitan Museum of Art, the largest art museum in the USA

Richardsonian Romanesque

Henry Hobson Richardson (1838–1886) became famous for a distinct type of architecture named Richardsonian Romanesque, seen in his amazing Trinity Church in Boston.

▶ Trinity Church shows the developing aesthetics of the USA. It stands on the same square as the Boston Public Library, a Beaux-Arts landmark

Art Nouveau

Art Nouveau is the name given to a decorative style that flourished for a brief period between 1890 and 1910. It was marked by the late 19th-century love for all things new and original. Architects of the time produced rich and flowing designs, deliberately free from historical influence. They created sinuous, asymmetrical, and swirling works using iron, glass, and other materials. Art Nouveau also affected interior design and commercial art (like poster and jewellery designs).

▲ *A bed and mirror by Gustave Serrurier-Bovy (1858–1910), the Belgian architect and furniture designer who pioneered the Art Nouveau style*

▲ *Maison Hankar, home of the early Art Nouveau architect Paul Hankar (1859–1901)*

▲ *This dragonfly corsage of gold, enamel and diamonds was made by René Lalique, one of Paris's leading Art Nouveau jewellery designers*

An International Theme

Art Nouveau is a French term. It began in England where it was inspired by Romantic literature and Pre-Raphaelite painters. The movement spread to other parts of Europe, developing regional variations. In Germany, the style was called *Jugendstil*; in Austria it was called *Sezessionstil*; in Italy it was called *Stile Floreale;* and in Spain, *Modernismo*.

▲ *The Peacock Room by James Whistler shows the burgeoning aesthetics of Art Nouveau*

Art Nouveau in France

The 1900 Paris Exposition held in the Beaux-Arts Grand Palais (*see pp 22*) exhibited a treasure-trove of Art Nouveau furniture, glassware, jewellery, and other decorative crafts. It made Paris the international centre for the Art Nouveau style. Soon, extraordinary new structures of iron, masonry, and concrete began to rise on the French landscape. This included the Paris Metro entrance gates designed by the influential young architect, Hector Guimard (1867–1942). Pioneering architect Anatole de Baudot (1834–1915) built the Church of Saint-Jean de Montmartre using reinforced concrete and steel rods; it was the first church to be constructed in this manner. Russian-born Parisian Xavier Schoellkopf (1869–1911) built a fabulous Art Nouveau house for the singer and actress, Yvette Guilbert. Even a Paris department store, La Samaritaine, was built in the new style, designed by Frantz Jourdain (1847–1935).

▲ *Wrought-iron Art Nouveau entrance of the Paris metro station*

▲ *Art Nouveau doorway by architect Jules Lavirotte (1864–1924) with sculptures by Jean-François Larrivé (1875–1928)*

Victor Horta (1861–1947)

The Belgian architect and designer Victor Horta is often considered the champion of the Art Nouveau movement. His earliest work in the style is the four-storied Hôtel Tassel (1892–1893) in Brussels. Its octagonal hall and curved staircase are characteristic of Art Nouveau. The architect's preference for such curvilinear and tendril-like forms is also seen in the sophisticated Hôtel Solvay, Hôtel van Eetvelde, and Horta's own home. His best-known work was the Maison du Peuple. It was the first building in Belgium to be designed with so much iron and glass on its facade. Sadly, this Art Nouveau gem was demolished in the 1965 to make way for a skyscraper.

▶ *The stairway at Hôtel Tassel*

Jugendstil and *Sezessionstil*

The flexible, S-shaped ornamental style, called whiplash or eel style, was common in *Jugendstil* and *Sezessionstil* designs. This can be seen in Munich's Hofatelier Elvira, created by August Endell (1871–1925) and Vienna's Majolikahaus, created by Otto Wagner (1841–1918). Wagner's student Josef Hoffmann designed Stoclet House in Brussels. This asymmetrical white masterpiece is now a UNESCO World Heritage Site. Eliel Saarinen brought Art Nouveau to Finland with his designs for the Helsinki Central Railway Station.

▶ *Whiplash motifs on the facade of Majolikahaus*

Defying Tradition

In the early 20th century, many architects came up with bold new designs that were inspired by traditional architecture, yet seemed to defy tradition. Some of these came from using modern materials like steel and concrete to build old designs like medieval towers and Classical arches. In many cases, the originality came by mixing different architectural traditions to create buildings of amazing originality.

▲ The Rashtrapati Bhavan (Presidential Palace) at New Delhi was designed in a mix of Indo-Saracenic and English Baroque architectural style by Edwin Lutyens (1869–1944)

▲ Designed by Jewish-German architect Erich Mendelsohn (1887–1953), the futuristic Einstein Tower in Potsdam was built over 1919–1921 to house a solar telescope. Einstein never worked here but is said to have approved of the brick and stucco structure as being organic

Karl Marx Hof

At the end of WWI, Vienna began building hordes of apartments for its impoverished working classes. The largest of these was the Karl Marx Hof, built over 1927–1930. Designed by the architect Karl Ehn, it stretched for 1.1 km and remains the longest single residential building in the world. The building held 1,382 apartments, plus laundromats, public baths, playschools, a library, a surgical clinic, and office spaces. Around it were playgrounds and gardens. The fortress-like building with its spikes and turrets became an actual holdout, when, in 1934, it became a battleground in the Austrian Civil War.

Incredible Individuals

In 1931, Germany was chosen to host the Olympic Games in 1936. Under orders from Hitler, architect Werner March and his brother Walter designed the gigantic Olympiastadion using a modern steel framework disguised in 'classical' stone. Hitler and his comrades watched the 1936 games from a special stand. His flawed beliefs in Aryan supremacy and Übermensch (Superhumans) were proven wrong before the whole world, when African American athlete Jesse Owens won four gold medals.

▲ Karl Marx Hof, designed in a rationalistic and functional style, is long that it spans four tram stops

▲ Olympiastadion, Berlin, 1936

MODERN ARCHITECTURE

Chilehaus

Built in what is called **Brick Expressionism**, Chilehaus is a massive 1920s office complex with 10 storeys. Designed by architect Fritz Höger (1877–1949) for a shipping magnate, the formidable building curves fluidly in the shape of a ship. The sharp angle at the tip—the nose of the 'ship'—is the most acute architectural bend in Europe. Occupying an incredible 5,950 m², Chilehaus is made of **reinforced concrete** and 4.8 million bricks. Because it is located on unstable land close to a river, the foundation had to be made secure. This was done by building concrete pilings that were 16 metres deep. Chilehaus has one of the few functioning **paternoster** lifts in the world.

In Real Life

At the age of 22, Jelisaveta Načić (1878–1955) became Serbia's first female architect. This was a time when women were discouraged from the profession. Despite all obstacles, she went on to become the chief architect for the Municipality of Belgrade. Among her brilliant and unique creations is the Alexander Nevsky Church (1929), built for monks who looked after wounded soldiers.

▲ The ship-shape, brick marvel of the 1920s, Chilehaus

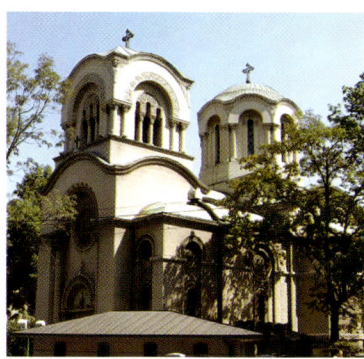
▲ Belgrade's Alexander Nevsky Church was inspired by a medieval Serbian style called the Morava school of architecture

Moscow Metro

Built on Stalin's orders, the Moscow metro stations are lavish constructions of marble, chandeliers, mosaics, and sculptures. Constructed underneath the city streets from the 1930s onwards, these ambitious projects showcase Russian architectural talent. The designs were guided by the principles of *svet* (light) and *sveltloe budushchee* (bright future). The station Ploshchad Revolyutsii, created by Alexey Dushkin, features 76 bronze sculptures. They depict Russian soldiers, farmers, workers, children, and famous individuals. The glittering Mayakovskaya station is famous for its 34 ceiling mosaics that show '24 Hours in the Land of the Soviets'. The white and gold Kievskaya station is dedicated to the friendship between Russia and Ukraine. It is named after Ukraine's capital, Kiev.

▲ The spectacular and futuristic Elektrozavodskaya station

▲ Social themes displayed in the art at Kievskaya station

Antoni Gaudí

The Spanish architect Antoni Gaudí i Cornet (1852–1926) had a unique style that defies categorisation. Gaudí loved the outdoors. Inspired by nature, he avoided designing buildings with straight lines. He analysed natural phenomena and living forms. Through this, he developed ways to build structures that curved and flowered in complex shapes. Such organic architecture had never been seen in the world before. Gaudí also decorated his creations with intense and symbolic details made from ceramics, tiles, stained glass, wrought-iron, and woodwork.

▲ The miraculous vaulted nave at the Sagrada Família, Gaudí's crowning achievement, symbolises trees rising up to the roof

▲ One of the painted, gated entrances at the fantastic Casa Milà, a UNESCO World Heritage Site

 ## Park Güell

Situated on top of a hill overlooking a sea, Park Güell was built over 1900–1914 as a private estate, and later opened to the public in 1926. This is one of Gaudí's early works in a naturalistic style. To build the park on the slopes, Gaudí analysed and invented amazing new geometrical solutions. This allowed him to make buildings in free-flowing designs that seemed one with nature. Gaudí's vivid imagination gave rise to many unique spaces, including undulating roads, a strangely tilted gallery, fairytale-like buildings by the entrance, an open hall with a forest of columns, and a number of statues, mosaics and fountains. Possibly the most popular spot is the main terrace, which is surrounded by a long bench shaped like a sea serpent.

▲ Park Guell's giant salamander mosaic nicknamed El Drac (The Dragon) is one of Gaudí's most well-known works

▲ Seen from the serpentine terrace, the whimsical buildings by the Park Guell entrance resemble gingerbread houses with meringue roofs and candied towers

▲ Unique, titled pillars support a road that follows the slope of a hill

MODERN ARCHITECTURE

Casa Batlló

Gaudí's Casa Batlló began as a renovation of an older, more conventional house that had four storeys. In the end, it transformed into a poetic, otherworldly construction. Gaudí changed the exterior by adding large oval windows on the first floor. Their frames are interrupted by long slender pillars in the shape of bones. Balconies on the floors above match this skeletal theme by resembling half-skulls with tilted openings for eyes. The entire bone-coloured facade is decorated with bright, multicoloured mosaics that resemble a lake of water lilies. Inside, Gaudí arranged the spaces and stairways to allow greater light and ventilation. The whole building is crowned with an amazing roof shaped like the back of a dragon resting against a stack of chimneys.

▲ The one-of-a-kind Casa Batlló

Incredible Individuals

A Roman Catholic, Gaudí held deep beliefs that he expressed in religious and symbolic imagery. He was also a kind human being who built schools and hospitals for his workers and their children. Under Pope John Paul II, Gaudí was officially named a 'Servant of God' in 2003.

◄ In 1902, Romantic artist Joan Llimona painted Saint Philip Neri using Gaudí as the model for the saint

▼ The spectacular Basilica of la Sagrada Família

Sagrada Família

The curvilinear Basilica of la Sagrada Família was Gaudí's last and greatest work. It was unfinished at the time of his death and is still under construction. Gaudí's design had 18 towers—12 representing the apostles, 4 for the evangelists, 1 for the Virgin Mary and 1 for Jesus Christ. The ornate Nativity facade, which faces the northeast, depicts the birth of Christ. It is surmounted by four towers of the apostles. The more austere Passion facade faces the setting sun and shows the suffering of Christ during the crucifixion. It bears the four other towers that have been constructed. Lifts inside the building take the visitors to the highest points.

Skyscrapers

The term 'skyscrapers' was first used during the 1880s. It was meant to describe buildings that were at least 10 storeys high. These first appeared in the USA. Early forms of the skyscraper were built with sturdy masonry at the ground level. This was later replaced by iron frameworks that could take the weight of higher floors. In the 1860s, a new way of processing steel—which is lighter and stronger than iron—led to the first true skyscrapers.

◀ The stylish Chrysler Building was the world's tallest building for a mere 11 months before the Empire State Building stole its limelight. The latter's architect sneakily bolted a spire on top of the Empire State Building to make it taller than the Chrysler. Here's an iconic image of a worker on the Empire State Building with the Chrysler Building behind him

▲ New York's Metropolitan Life Insurance Building (1909) was designed by Napoleon Le Brun after St Mark's Campanile, a famous bell tower in Venice

Elevators

A number of technological and social changes brought the skyscraper into existence. Key among them was the invention of the safety elevator, by Elisha Otis, in the mid-19th century. The safety feature allowed the lift to carry passengers safely, without the fear of cables breaking. The first safety elevator was installed in the E.V. Haughwout & Co. store, New York, in 1857. It was powered by steam, not electricity. And it was effective for buildings that were only about 4–5 storeys high.

Isn't It Amazing!

While skyscrapers were multiplying rapidly in 19th-century Chicago and New York, things were a little different in London. Queen Victoria had complained that tall buildings obstructed the view. Thus, architects were forced to stick to lower heights. This rule continues to exist today, with a few exceptions.

▲ London's first skyscraper, 55 Broadway, was built by architect Charles Holden. Constructed over 1927–1929, it was the new HQ for the electric railways and still houses the Transport for London offices

◀ Elisha Otis demonstrated the safety elevator at the 1853 World's Fair held in New York's Crystal Palace

Early Skyscrapers

One of the earliest buildings to use a metal framework was Oriel Chambers (1864) in Liverpool, England. Designed by Peter Ellis, it was five floors high and featured a glass **curtain wall**. The first skyscraper to use a steel frame was William Le Baron Jenney's 10-storey-high Home Insurance Building (1884–1885) in Chicago. It was soon followed by Burnham and Root's 45-metre-high, all-steel Rand McNally Building (1889) in the same city. In St. Louis, Missouri, the 10-storey-high Wainwright Building (1891) was designed by Dankmar Adler and Louis Sullivan. Its honeycomb of office windows were separated by vertical shafts inspired by Classical architecture. This design emphasized the soaring nature of the skyscraper. It is considered the father of modern-day office buildings.

▲ Oriel Chambers with its glass curtain wall

Flatiron Building

The triangular, 22-storey Flatiron Building in New York is one of the most dramatic landmarks of the city. It was designed by Chicago architect and urban planner Daniel Burnham (1846–1912) and designer Frederick P. Dinkelberg. Construction was completed in 1902. With a terracotta and limestone facade, the building has a Beaux-Arts style with French and Renaissance influences. The narrow end of the triangle is less than 2 metre wide.

In Real Life

The 102-storey Empire State Building was designed by the architectural firm Shreve, Lamb & Harmon. When it was completed in 1931, the building was 381 metre high. When its antenna was added in 1950, the total height came up to 449 metre, but reduced to 443 metre when the antenna was replaced. It was the tallest building in the world for 40 years until the World Trade Centre was built.

▲ The Empire State Building as seen from across the East River

▲ The Flatiron Building towering over Manhattan

Word Check

Age of Reason: It is also called the Age of Enlightenment; this was an intellectual and philosophical movement in 18th-century Europe.

Arabesque: It is a form of decoration made of scrolling, interlacing tendrils, foliage or plain lines.

Baltic States: It is the combined name for three independent nations on the eastern coast of the Baltic Sea—Estonia, Latvia, and Lithuania.

Brick Expressionism: A style of architecture that used bricks and tiles; it existed during the 1920s around Germany and the Netherlands.

Byzantine: It is anything relating to Byzantium, a Christian empire of medieval times that centred on the city of Constantinople, which is now modern-day Istanbul.

Cossack Hetmanate: 'Cossack' means 'free man' and 'Hetman' means 'headman'. The Cossack Hetmanate was the government of an independent 17th or 18th-century nation that became modern Ukraine.

Curtain wall: On a building, this is an outer layer of any material (stone or glass or iron) that carries only its own weight. It is often used for decorative impact.

Hellenist: It is anything relating to ancient Greek culture, especially between 4th–1st century BCE.

Manueline: It is a lavish, decorative style of architecture that existed in Portugal during the 16th century during (and just after) the reign of King Manuel I.

Ottoman Empire: Between the 14th and 20th centuries, great swathes of southeast Europe, northwest Asia, and northern Africa were controlled by Turkish emperors called the Ottomans.

Reinforced concrete: It is concrete that is reinforced by another material, usually steel bars embedded into the concrete.

Relief: It is a sculpture that is attached to walls so that it rises from or above the wall surface.

Renaissance: It refers to the period of revival of Classical (ancient Greek and Roman) art and architecture during the 14th to 16th centuries. It began in Italy and spread to the rest of Europe.

Paternoster: In buildings, a paternoster is a type of lift with many open compartments travelling up and down on a conveyor-belt-like mechanism. The compartments do not stop at the floor, but they travel slowly, so you can just jump off at the right floor, while it keeps moving upwards/downwards.

Stucco: It is a fine plaster that is used to coat walls or sometimes mould into decorative forms.

Turreted: A building that has a turret (a small tower on top of a larger tower or building).